Curries
– Delectable and Mouth-watering
From the West India

By

Aroona Reejhsinghani

V&S PUBLISHERS

Published by:

V&S PUBLISHERS

F-2/16, Ansari Road, Daryaganj, New Delhi-110002
☎ 011-23240026, 011-23240027 • *Fax:* 011-23240028
Email: info@vspublishers.com • *Website:* www.vspublishers.com

Regional Office : Hyderabad
5-1-707/1, Brij Bhawan (Beside Central Bank of India Lane)
Bank Street, Koti, Hyderabad - 500 095
☎ 040-24737290
E-mail: vspublishershyd@gmail.com

Branch Office : Mumbai
Jaywant Industrial Estate, 2nd Floor–222, Tardeo Road
Opposite Sobo Central Mall, Mumbai – 400 034
☎ 022-23510736
E-mail: vspublishersmum@gmail.com

Follow us on:

All books available at **www.vspublishers.com**

CONTENTS

INTRODUCTION

India is famous for its curries. In fact, it is the home of an endless variety of curries, each better than the other. Indians relish hundreds of curries made with vegetables, meat, fish, prawn and eggs. Every Zone in India has its own special way of preparing curries, therefore, each curry has a unique flavour.

In India, majority of the people are vegetarian, hence there is a greater variety of delicious vegetarian curries prepared with dals and a variety of vegetables, curds and buttermilk. But this does not mean that there is very little to choose in case of non-vegetarian curries. Indian meat curries, in fact, take many forms. Like kofta curries, ground meat is shaped into balls and cooked in a deliciously rich sauce or curry. Then, there are korma curries — spicy and delicious, keema curries — which is ground meat cooked with peas and decorated with hard-boiled eggs.

In this book, I have chosen for you a wide variety of flavours — some simple, some exotic, some extraordinarily delicious. This book contains recipes for some special curries made and enjoyed in West Zone of India. The aim is to make people relish curries of a particular region even if they don't belong to that region. Even the foreigners can try these recipes to relish a unique taste. Here for you is a distinctive selection of curries which are as distinctive as different wines in different bottles.

Aroona Reejhsinghani
502 B, Lila Apts.
opp. Gul Mohar Gardens,
Yari Road, Versova
Bombay-61
Ph – 6360224

1

MAHARASHTRIAN CURRIES

Marathis are simple, hard-working and unassuming. Therefore their eating habits are also simple. Every morning one finds the lady of the house busy grinding coconut and other spices on the grinding stone. Although it is a laborious task, Marathi women do not mind it because without the addition of coconut and hot and spicy condiments no Marathi curry is said to be complete. Marathis are very fond of fish and shellfish, therefore prawn and fish curry take a place of pride on their menu. Pomfret and bangda are the most popular fishes of Maharashtra. Maharashtrians are so obsessed with fish that they buy fish and dry it in the sun in summer so that they can have fish curry in the monsoons and also when heavy rains prevent the fishermen from bringing in the fresh catch.

Non-Vegetarian Curries
Spicy Pomfret Curry

Ingredients (Serves 4)

- 1 pomfret, cleaned and cut into slices
- 1/4 coconut
- 4 green chillies
- 1-inch piece of ginger
- 4 flakes of garlic
- 1/2 small bunch of coriander leaves
- 1/2 tsp. turmeric powder
- 1 small ball of tamarind
- 1/2 tblsp. ground cumin seeds
- 1/2 tblsp. ground coriander seeds
- Salt and chilli powder to taste

Preparation

Soak tamarind in $1\frac{1}{2}$ cup hot water for 5 minutes then squeeze out the juice, grind the remaining ingredients to a paste and apply paste on the fish. Heat 3 tblsps. oil and fry the fish nicely then pour in the tamarind water and cook till the gravy is a little thick.

Fish And Potato Curry

Ingredients (Serves 5)

- 1 medium pomfret, cleaned and sliced
- 2 medium potatoes, peeled and diced into cubes
- 1 big onion, minced
- 1/4 tsp. turmeric powder
- 1 tblsp. dhania-jeera powder
- 1/4 coconut
- 2 big tomatoes, pureed
- 4 green chillies, slit
- A few curry leaves
- 2 tblsps. tamarind water
- Salt and chilli powder to taste

Preparation

Grind coconut to a paste. Heat 3 tblsps. oil and fry the onions till they become soft. Add tomatoes, coconut, spices and chillies. When the tomatoes turn soft, add potatoes, pour in two cups of water and cook till the potatoes are half done. Lightly fry the fish and add to the curry. Add curry leaves and tamarind. Cook till the potatoes and fish are done. Decorate with coriander leaves.

Bangda Curry

Ingredients (Serves 6)

- 1 dozen bangda fish
- 1/4 coconut
- 6 green chillies
- 8 flakes of garlic
- 1 lime-sized ball of tamarind
- 4 flakes of garlic, sliced finely
- Handful of coriander leaves
- 1/4 tsp. turmeric powder
- 1 tblsp. dhania-jeera powder
- Salt and chilli powder to taste

Preparation

Cut the fishes after cleaning them into small pieces. Apply on the cut pieces salt, chilli, and turmeric powder. Soak tamarind in two cups of water for 5 minutes and then squeeze out the juice. Grind coconut, chillies and whole flakes of garlic to a paste. Heat 4 tblsps. oil and fry the sliced garlic to a red colour. Add to it fish and fry a little, then add ground paste and spices, mix well. Now pour in the tamarind water. Cook till done. Serve decorated with chopped coriander leaves.

PRAWN CURRY

Ingredients (Serves 4)

- 500 grams prawns, cleaned and deveined
- 1/2 tsp. turmeric powder
- 1/2 coconut
- 1 tsp. coriander seeds
- 6 red chillies
- 1 small onion
- 1/2 cup tamarind water
- Handful of coriander leaves
- 2 medium onions minced
- 1 tsp. ground cumin seeds
- Salt and chilli powder to taste

Preparation

Apply salt and turmeric on prawns and set aside for half an hour. Grind coconut, small onion, coriander and cumin seeds and chillies to a paste. Heat 4 tblsps. oil and fry onions till soft. Add prawns and fry till they turn dry. Pour in 1 cup water with tamarind and cook till the prawns are almost done, then put in the ground paste and cook till prawns are done. Serve decorated with coriander leaves.

PRAWNS AND VEGETABLE CURRY

Ingredients (Serves 8)

- 500 grams prawns, shelled and deveined
- 2 medium onions, minced
- 2 medium potatoes, peeled and cubed
- 250 grams peas, shelled
- 1 small brinjal, diced
- 1 drumstick, scraped and cut into 1-inch pieces
- 2 medium tomatoes, blanched and sliced
- 8 cocums
- 4 green chillies
- 1 small bunch of coriander leaves
- 1/4 coconut
- 1 tblsp. each of grated garlic and ginger
- 1 tsp. each of garam masala and turmeric powder
- 2 tblsp. dhania-jeera powder
- Salt and chilli powder to taste

Preparation

Grind chillies, coriander leaves, coconut, garlic and ginger to a paste. Apply salt and turmeric on prawns and set aside for half an hour. Clean and wash the cocums. Heat 5 tblsps. oil and fry the onions till soft. Add prawns and fry till dry. Then mix in the vegetables, ground coconut paste, salt and spices. When the vegetables are almost done, put in tomatoes and cocums. When the vegetables are cooked, remove from fire and decorate with coriander leaves.

PRAWN AND PUMPKIN CURRY

Ingredients (Serves 8)

- 500 grams prawns, shelled and deveined
- 500 grams red or white pumpkin, diced
- 6 red chillies
- 1 tsp. fenugreek seeds
- 1 tblsp coriander seeds
- 1 medium onion
- 1 small onion, finely sliced
- A few curry leaves
- 6 flakes of garlic
- 1/2 tsp. turmeric powder
- 1 tsp. cumin seeds
- 1/2 coconut
- 1 lime-sized ball of tamarind
- Salt to taste

Preparation

Fry all the spices, coconut, whole onion and garlic to a red colour and grind to a paste. Cover tamarind with 1 cup hot water for 5 minutes and then squeeze out the juice. Heat 4 tblsps. oil and fry prawns till dry. Put in the pumpkin and 2 cups water and salt and cook till the prawns are almost done. Put in the tamarind and coconut paste and continue cooking till the prawns are done. Remove from fire. Heat 1 tblsp. oil and fry curry leaves and sliced onion nicely and pour it over the curry.

MUTTON CURRY

Ingredients (Serves 4)

- 500 grams mutton, cut into serving portions
- 3 medium onions, grated
- 1 tblsp. each of ground ginger and garlic
- 6 red chillies
- 1 tblsp. peppercorns
- 1/2 tsp. turmeric powder
- 1/2 dry coconut
- 1 large onion
- 1-inch piece cinnamon stick
- 1 tblsp. poppy seeds
- 4 cardamoms, 4 cloves
- Salt and chilli powder to taste

Preparation

Grind chillies, mix them with ginger, salt and turmeric powder and apply the mixture on the mutton. Set it aside for 1 hour. Roast coconut and 1 big onion on fire till red and grind to a paste along with poppy seeds and whole spices. Heat 5 tblsps. ghee and fry onions till brown, add mutton and fry to a golden colour. Mix in the coconut paste and cover with hot water. Cook till the mutton is tender. Decorate with coriander leaves.

CHICKEN AND PEAS CURRY

Ingredients (Serves 6)

- 1 medium chicken, disjointed
- 250 grams peas
- 125 grams onions, finely sliced
- 8 flake garlic
- A 2-inch piece of ginger
- 8 green chillies
- 1 tsp. garam masala
- 1 tblsp dhania-jeera powder
- 1/8 tsp. each of grated nutmeg and mace
- Handful of coriander leaves
- 1/2 tsp. turmeric powder
- 250 grams beaten curd
- 3 cups thin and 1 cup thick coconut milk
- 25 grams cashewnuts
- Salt and chilli powder to taste

Preparation

Grind ginger, garlic and chillies to a paste. Mix the paste into curd along with all the spices, salt and chicken and set aside for 1 hour. Heat 6 tblsps. oil and fry onions to a red colour. Then add chicken and fry it to a red colour. Add cashewnuts and pour in thin coconut milk. Cook over a slow fire till the chicken turns almost tender. Add peas and thick milk. Simmer over a slow fire till the chicken turns soft. Decorate with coriander leaves.

2

GUJARATI CURRIES

Since a large number of Gujaratis are vegetarian, it is not surprising to find that they prepare some of the most delicious vegetarian curries. Among the most popular Gujarati curries are sweet and sour curry and buttermilk curry. Gujaratis have endless ways of preparing curries, each different and tantalizing.

Vegetarian Curries
Lady's Finger Curry

Ingredients (Serves 4)

- 250 grams lady's fingers (bhendi), slit lengthwise, but not halved
- 1 glass buttermilk
- 2 tblsps. gramflour or besan
- 1/2 tsp. turmeric powder
- 1/2 tblsp. grated ginger
- 4 green chillies
- 1 small bunch of coriander leaves
- 4 flakes of garlic
- 1 small onion
- 1 tblsp. dhania-jeera powder
- Salt and chilli powder to taste

Preparation

Grind ginger, chillies, coriander leaves, onion and garlic to a paste. Mix the paste with spices and salt, and stuff it into each bhendi. Dissolve gramflour in buttermilk. Heat 3 tblsps. oil and fry the vegetable nicely. Put in buttermilk, salt and turmeric powder. Cook over a slow fire till the curry turns a little thick. Serve decorated with chopped coriander.

CORN CURRY

Ingredients (Serves 5)

- 4 corn cobs, 1 glass buttermilk
- 25 grams cashewnuts
- 1/4 dry coconut
- 2 medium onions
- 1/2 tsp. each of grated ginger and garlic
- 5 green chillies
- 2 medium potatoes, boiled, peeled and cubed
- 1 small bunch of coriander leaves
- 1/2 tsp. each of turmeric powder and garam masala
- 1 tsp. dhania-jeera powder
- Salt and chilli powder to taste

Preparation

Roast the coconut and grind it to a paste along with ginger, garlic, chillies, cashewnuts, onions and coriander leaves. Deep fry the potatoes to a golden colour. Heat 3 tblsps. oil and fry the ground paste till the oil floats out. Then put in the corn, all the spices and salt. Pour in the buttermilk and cook over a slow fire till the corn is done. Then put in the potatoes. Cook for a few more minutes and serve decorated with chopped coriander leaves.

CARROT KOFTA CURRY

Ingredients (Serves 6)

For Curry

- 2 big tomatoes, grated
- 1/4 coconut
- 1 tblsp. poppy seeds
- 2 tblsps. curd
- 10 cashewnuts
- 1 tsp. each of ginger and garlic paste
- 1 small onion
- 4 green chillies
- 1 small bunch of coriander leaves
- 1/2 tsp. each of turmeric powder and garam masala
- 1 tblsp garam masala
- Salt, sugar and chilli powder to taste

For Koftas

- 500 grams grated carrots
- 2 tblsps. gramflour
- 1 small bunch of coriander leaves
- 2 green chillies, minced
- 1 tsp. grated ginger
- 1 tsp. ground cumin seeds
- Raisins
- A few sliced mint leaves
- Salt and chilli powder to taste

Preparation

Grind ginger, chillies, mint and coriander leaves coarsely. Squeeze out all the moisture from carrots. Mix all the kofta ingredients except raisins. Form the carrots into oblong-shaped balls around a raisin. Deep fry the carrots to a golden colour. To prepare curry, grind coconut, poppy seeds, ginger, garlic and onions to a paste. Heat 3 tblsps. oil and fry the paste till the oil comes out. Put in all the spices, tomatoes, sugar and curds. Cook till dry. Put in 3 cups of water, boil for 5 minutes. Pour the curry over koftas and serve decorated with coriander leaves.

Brinjal Curry

Ingredients (Serves 4)

- 250 grams small brinjals
- 2 tblsps. gramflour dissolved in 1 glass sour buttermilk
- 4 green chillies, slit
- 1/2 tsp. cumin seeds
- Handful of coriander leaves
- Pinch of asafoetida
- 1/2 tsp. each of turmeric powder and garam masala
- 1 tsp. dhania-jeera powder
- Salt and chilli powder to taste

Preparation

Cut the brinjals into fours halfway through. Mix all the spices with salt and stuff into the brinjals. Heat 3 tblsps. oil and add asafoetida and cumin seeds. When the seeds stop popping, put in the brinjals and fry for 5 minutes, then pour in the buttermilk. Add sugar and chillies and cook till the brinjals are done. Serve decorated with coriander leaves.

BUTTERMILK CURRY

Ingredients (Serves 5)

- 2 glasses sour buttermilk
- 2 tblsps. gramflour
- 1 tblsp. grated jaggery
- 1/2 tsp. turmeric powder
- 1 tblsp. dhania-jeera powder
- A few curry leaves
- 1/4 tsp. each of mustard, cumin and fenugreek seeds
- 1 onion, grated
- 1 tsp. each of grated ginger and garlic
- 3 green chillies, slit
- 2 red chillies, broken into bits
- Salt to taste

Preparation

Mix buttermilk with gramflour, salt and all the spices. Heat 2 tblsps. oil and add a pinch of hing, mustard, cumin and fenugreek seeds and red chillies. Fry till the mixture turns brown. Add ginger, garlic, onion and curry leaves and cook till soft. Put in buttermilk along with remaining ingredients and cook till the curry turns a little thick. Serve hot.

Mukund Curry

Ingredients (Serves 4)

- 1-1/2 cups wheat flour
- 250 grams peas
- 100 grams tomatoes, grated
- 1 tsp. each of grated ginger and garlic
- Pinch of baking soda
- 2 bay leaves
- 1 glass sour buttermilk
- 1 tblsp dhania-jeera powder
- 1/2 tsp. each of garam masala and turmeric powder
- Handful of coriander leaves.
- 4 green chillies, slit
- 2 medium onions
- Salt and chilli powder to taste

Preparation

Mix together flour and salt. Rub in 1 tblsp ghee, and add enough water to form a stiff dough. Wash the dough in a bowl of water till the dough turns milky white. Remove the dough from water, mix in soda and flatten the dough to a thin round cake. Steam it till it turns spongy. Cut into small pieces and fry to a golden colour. Grind ginger, garlic onions to a paste. Heat 2 tblsps. oil and fry the paste along with the bay leaves till the oil comes out. Add all the spices, salt, tomatoes and peas. When the tomatoes turn soft, add buttermilk and chillies and fried pieces. Cook over a slow fire for 5 minutes. Serve decorated with coriander leaves.

POTATO KOFTA CURRY

Ingredients (Serves 4)

For Curry

- 2 small tomatoes, grated
- 250 grams beaten curd
- 1 cup coconut milk
- 1/2 tsp. each of turmeric powder and garam masala
- 1 tblsp dhania-jeera powder
- 4 green chillies, slit
- 2 medium onions
- 1 tsp. each of ginger and garlic paste
- A pinch of asafoetida
- A few curry leaves

For Koftas

- 2 big potatoes, boiled and peeled
- 1 slice of bread, soaked in water and squeezed dry
- 2 green chillies, minced
- Handful of coriander leaves
- 1 tsp. crushed pomegranate seeds
- 1/2 tsp. turmeric powder
- 50 grams gramflour
- A pinch of baking soda
- 1 tsp. ground cumin seeds

Preparation

Mix cumin powder, turmeric powder, salt and soda into the flour. Add enough water to form a thick batter. Mix potatoes with chillies, bread, pomegranate seeds and then form the mixture into small balls. Dip the balls in batter and deep fry them to a golden colour. Beat curd with 2 cups of water. Grind ginger, garlic and onions to a paste. Heat 3 tblsp. oil and fry the paste till the oil comes out. Add tomatoes, all the spices, curd, curry leaves and chillies. When the mixture turns dry, add pakodas and then coconut milk. Simmer for 5-7 mins. Serve decorated with coriander leaves.

Tomato Curry

Ingredients (Serves 6)

- 500 grams tomatoes, grated
- 2 cups thin and 1 cup thick coconut milk
- A few curry and coriander leaves
- 1/2 tsp. each of turmeric powder and garam masala
- 1 tblsp. dhania-jeera powder
- 1 tsp. each of grated ginger and garlic
- 1 medium onion, grated
- 4 green chillies, slit
- A pinch of asafoetida
- 1 tblsp. gramflour
- 1/4 tsp. each of mustard and cumin seeds
- 1 tblsp. sugar
- Salt to taste

Preparation

Mix gramflour in thin coconut milk. Heat 3 tblsps. oil and add hing, cumin and mustard seeds. When the seeds stop popping, add ginger, garlic and onion. Fry till soft, then put in tomatoes, curry leaves, all the spices, salt and sugar. Cook till the oil oozes out, then pour in thin milk and chillies. When the curry turns a little thick, pour in thick coconut milk and remove the curry from fire. Decorate with coriander leaves.

SWEET AND SOUR CURRY

Ingredients (Serves 5)

- 250 grams arhar or tuvar dal
- 50 grams each of suran, red pumpkin and doodhi
- 50 grams potatoes, brinjals and one raw banana
- 4 big tomatoes, grated
- 1 tblsp. grated jaggery
- 2 tblsps. thick tamarind juice
- A few curry leaves
- 1 big onion, grated; 1 tsp. grated ginger
- Handful of chopped coriander leaves
- A pinch of asafoetida
- 1/4 tsp. each of mustard and cumin seeds
- 1 tblsp. til
- 1 tblsp. grated coconut
- 1/2 tsp. turmeric powder
- 2 red and 2 green chillies
- Salt to taste

Preparation

Wash and soak dal in water for 1 hour. Drain and boil in water to which turmeric and salt has been added. When dal becomes soft, mash it to a paste. Heat 3 tblsps. oil, add mustard, cumin seeds and asafeotida. When the seeds stop popping, add ginger, onions, chillies and curry leaves and cook till soft. Cut all the vegetables, into 1-inch pieces and set aside. Put tomatoes into the onions and cook till the mixture becomes thick, then put in the vegetables, dal, tamarind, jaggery and 1 litre water. Cook till the vegetables are done. Sprinkle on top roasted til, coconut and coriander leaves. Serve hot.

3

SINDHI CURRIES

Since Sindhis lived under Muslim rule for centuries, Muslim influence on their food is predominant. It is not therefore surprising that some of their curries, specially the non-vegetarian ones, have Persian influence. But this does not mean that they do not have their own distinctive curries. Today Sindhi curry, which is made in different ways with varying ingredients, is enjoyed by people of various castes and creeds throughout India.

Vegetarian Curries

Giantha Curry

Ingredients (Serves 5)

For Gianthas

- 200 grams gramflour or besan
- 1 tblsp. each of pomegranate and cumin seeds
- 4 green chillies, minced
- 1/2 tsp. ginger, minced
- 1 tblsp ghee
- Salt and chilli powder to taste

For Curry

- 1 large onion, minced
- 1/2 tsp. each of grated ginger and garlic
- 4 green chillies, minced
- 2 tblsps. mango powder
- 1 tblsp. coriander powder
- 1/2 tsp. each of turmeric powder and garam masala
- 1/2 tsp. each of cumin and mustard seeds
- A few sprigs of coriander leaves
- Salt to taste

Preparation

Mix together all the ingredients of gianthas. Add enough water to form a stiff dough. Roll the dough into a 1/4 inch thick sheet. Cut the sheet into long strips and each strip into 1-inch square pieces. Boil the gianthas in water for 20 minutes. Heat 3 tblsps. oil and fry onions, ginger, garlic and chillies till soft. Add gianthas along with the water in which they were boiled, spices and salt. Cook for a few minutes. Heat 1 tblsp. oil and fry mustard and cumin seeds. Put this oil over the curry and decorate with coriander leaves.

Giantha and Spinach Curry

For giantha ingredients and method of giantha preparation, refer to the recipe *'Giantha Curry'*

Ingredients (Serves 4)

- 2 bunches of spinach, finely chopped
- 1 small onion, minced
- 1 tsp. each of ginger and garlic paste
- 4 green chillies, minced
- 1 tblsp. dhania-jeera powder
- 1/4 tsp. turmeric powder
- 100 grams grated tomatoes
- 6 flakes of garlic crushed
- Salt and chilli powder to taste

Preparation

Heat 3 tblsps. oil and fry onions, ginger and garlic paste and chillies till soft. Add spinach, spices, tomatoes and salt. Cook till spinach is soft. Mash the spinach mixture to a paste, add 2 cups of water and gianthas. Cook till the curry turns a little thick. Fry crushed garlic in 2 tblsps. ghee and pour the ghee over the curry.

VEGETABLE CURRY NO. 1

Ingredients (Serves 6)

- 125 grams gramflour
- 2 drumsticks, scraped and cut into big pieces
- 2 medium sized tindas, scraped and cut into quarters
- 2 medium sized potatoes, peeled and quartered
- 100 grams lady's fingers
- 50 grams each of french beans and guvar
- 1 brinjal, sliced
- 1/8 tsp. asafoetida
- 1/2 tsp. each of mustard, cumin and fenugreek seeds
- 100 grams tomatoes, grated
- 1 tsp. turmeric powder
- A few curry leaves, 1 tsp. green chilli paste
- 12-15 cocums, 1 tsp. ginger paste
- Salt to taste

Preparation

Heat 5 tblsps. oil and fry the gramflour to a golden colour. Heat 2 tblsps. oil and add asafoetida and all the seeds. When the seeds stop popping, add tomatoes, curry leaves and remaining spices. When oil oozes out, add ginger and chilli paste and all the vegetables. Fry the mixture for a few minutes. Dissolve gramflour in 1 litre water and put it in the fried mixture. Add cocums, cook till the vegetables are done and the curry is a little thick.

Vegetable Curry No. 2

Ingredients (Serves 6)

- 125 grams tuvar dal
- 3 tblsps. gramflour
- Rest of the ingredients are same as mentioned in *'Vegetable Curry No. 1''*

Preparation

Boil the dal in water with salt and turmeric powder till soft. Mash the soft dal and pass it through a sieve. Dissolve gramflour in 1 litre water and pour into mashed dal. Heat 4 tblsps. ghee and add asafoetida and all the seeds. When the seeds stop popping, add tomatoes, spices and curry leaves. Let the tomatoes turn soft, then add all the vegetables and fry for a few minutes. Now put in the dal-gramflour water along with cocums. Cook till the vegetables are done and the curry turns a little thick.

NON-VEGETARIAN CURRIES

SHAHI KOFTA CURRY

Ingredients (Serves 2)

For Koftas

- 250 grams kheema or minced mutton
- 1 small onion, minced
- 3 flakes of garlic, minced
- 1/2 tsp. garam masala and cardamom seeds
- Handful of coriander leaves
- 2 green chillies, 6 mint leaves
- Salt to taste.

For Curry

- 100 grams onions, grated
- 1 tsp. grated ginger
- 4 green chillies, minced
- 100 grams tomatoes, grated
- 1 tsp. each of ground cumin seeds and garam masala
- 125 grams sour curd
- Salt and chilli powder to taste

Preparation

Grind all the kofta ingredients to a paste. Form the paste into round balls. Melt 3 tblsps. ghee in a pan, spread the koftas in it. Cover the pan, sprinkle a little cold water on the lid and cook over a slow fire till the koftas are dry. Heat 4 tblsps. ghee and fry onions, ginger and chillies till they turn soft. Then add tomatoes, all the spices, curd and salt. When the ghee oozes out, add the koftas. Pour in 2 cups of water, bring the mixture to a boil and remove it from fire. Decorate with coriander leaves.

DILPASAND KOFTA CURRY

Ingredients (Serves 2)

For Curry

- 2 medium onions, grated,
- 1 tsp. each of ginger and garlic paste
- 2 medium potatoes, boiled, peeled and quartered
- Salt and chilli powder to taste
- 1 tsp. each of coriander and cumin seeds
- 1 tsp. garam masala
- 2 red and 2 green chillies, minced
- 100 grams tomatoes, grated
- 250 grams lotus stems or bhien, cleaned, sliced and boiled

For Koftas

- 250 grams kheema
- 1 beaten egg
- Handful of coriander leaves
- 8 mint leaves
- 4 green chillies
- 1 small onion
- 1 tsp. coriander powder
- 1/2 tsp. garam masala
- 1 tsp. grated ginger
- 1 cup fine bread crumbs
- Salt and chilli powder to taste

Preparation

Boil kheema in salted water till it becomes tender and dry. Mix in kheema and rest of the kofta ingredients. Form the mixture into round balls or koftas, roll the balls in crumbs. Deep fry the balls to a golden colour. Grind onion, ginger and garlic to a paste. Heat 4 tblsps. ghee and fry the ground paste till soft. Add tomatoes, coriander leaves, chillies, all the spices and salt. Cook the mixture till the oil oozes out. Then put in 2 cups of water, potatoes and bhien. Cook for 5 minutes and pour the curry over the koftas. Sprinkle garam masala on top and serve hot.

Mutton and Vegetable Curry

Ingredients (Serves 4)

- 500 grams mutton, cut into serving portions
- 250 grams onions, grated
- 1 tblsps. each of grated ginger and garlic
- 100 grams grated tomatoes
- 2 tblsps. coriander powder
- 1 tblsp. garam masala
- 100 grams sour curd
- 1 tsp. ground cumin seeds
- 4 green chillies, minced
- 2 medium-sized potatoes, peeled and quartered
- 250 grams lotus stems or bhien, cleaned , sliced and boiled
- 2 medium-sized tindas or white gourds, scraped and quartered
- Handful of coriander leaves
- Salt and chilli powder to taste
- 4 tblsps. brandy or whisky

Preparation

Heat 100 grams ghee and fry onions, ginger and garlic to a golden colour. Add mutton and fry to a golden colour also. Add tomatoes, spices, green chillies, curd and salt. Cook the contents till ghee comes on top, then put in all the vegetables and one glass of water and brandy. Finish cooking when both vegetables and mutton are done. Serve decorated with coriander leaves.

4

GOAN CURRIES

Goa is a tiny island lying between the Arabian Sea and the Western Ghats. Since it is skirted by the sea, it has been bestowed with abundant varieties of fish and shellfish. Goans prepare many delicious fish curries. Today throughout India, people enjoy Goan fish and prawn curries. Having lived under Portuguese rule for over 450 years, the food of Goans is a mixture of both Eastern and Western influences. Goans excel in culinary art and they make such fine chefs that most of the leading hotels in India are served by Goan chefs.

Non-Vegetarian Curries
Spicy Fish Curry

Ingredients (Serves 4)

- 1 medium white fleshed fish, cleaned and sliced
- 1 tblsp. each of cumin seeds, coriander and poppy seeds.
- 1 tblsp. rice
- Handful of coriander leaves
- Refined flour
- 1 tblsp. grated ginger
- 12 cashewnuts, 1 tblsp. peppercorns
- 2 medium onions, finely sliced
- A big pinch of sugar
- 1/2 coconut, 6 flakes of garlic
- 4 green chillies, slit
- 4 medium tomatoes, pureed
- 1/2 tsp. turmeric powder
- Salt and chilli powder to taste

Preparation

Apply salt and turmeric powder on fish and set it aside for half an hour. Roll fish lightly in flour and fry to a golden colour. Grind coriander, cumin and poppy seeds, peppercorns, rice, coconut and cashewnuts to paste. Extract juice — this is known as thick milk. Pour 2 cups hot water over the squeezed out pulp and set it aside for 15 minutes, then squeeze the pulp dry — this is known as thin milk. Heat 3 tblsps. oil and fry onions, ginger and chillies till soft. Then put in remaining spices, tomatoes, salt and sugar. Cook till oil comes out, then put in fish and thin milk. Cook for 5 minutes, and pour in thick milk. Heat the curry to simmering and serve decorated with coriander leaves.

POMFRET CURRY

Ingredients (Serves 4)

- 1 medium pomfret, cleaned and sliced
- 1/2 coconut,
- 6 red chillies, few curry leaves
- 2 tblsps. each of coriander and poppy seeds
- 1 large onion, 1 tsp. cumin seeds
- 4 green chillies, slit
- 3 cocums, 10 cashewnuts
- 6 flakes of garlic
- 1 lime-sized ball of tamarind
- Salt to taste

Preparation

Apply salt and turmeric on fish and set it aside for half an hour. Then fry the fish lightly. Roast together onion, red chillies, garlic, coconut, coriander, cumin, poppy seeds and cashewnuts along with tamarind, and grind the mixture to a paste. Heat 3 tblsps. of oil and fry the paste nicely, adding water from time to time till a nice aroma comes out of the mixture. Then pour in 3 cups of water and add cocums. Bring the mixture to a boil and put in fish and cook for 5-7 minutes. Decorate with chopped coriander leaves.

Fish and Brinjal Curry

Ingredients (Serves 6)

- 1 pomfret or any other white-fleshed fish, cleaned
- 250 grams brinjals, cut into long finger-like slices
- 1 lime-sized ball of tamarind
- 1 tblsp. mustard seeds
- 1 big onion, sliced
- 1 tblsp. each of coriander and poppy seeds
- 1/2 tsp. turmeric powder, 1 tsp. cumin seeds
- 1 tblsp. each of grated ginger and garlic
- 6 red chillies
- 1 medium onion
- 1/2 coconut
- Salt to taste

Preparation

Apply salt and turmeric powder on slices of fish and set them aside for half an hour. Roast together coriander, cumin and poppy seeds, 1 medium onion, ginger, garlic, chillies and coconut. Grind this mixture to a fine paste. Fry the fish lightly in oil. Soak tamarind in one cup hot water and then squeeze out the juice. Heat 3 tblsps. oil and put in the mustard seeds, when the seeds stop popping, put in the sliced onion and fry till soft. Then put in the ground paste and fry nicely. Add brinjals, mix well, add tamarind and 3 cups of water. When the brinjals are almost done, put in the fish. Remove the curry from fire when the brinjals are done.

Pork Curry

Ingredients (Serves 8)

- 1 kilo pork, cut into serving portions
- 5 large onions, minced
- 1/2 tsp. turmeric powder
- 2 tblsps. dhania-jeera powder
- 2-inch piece of cinnamon stick
- 8 cloves, 8 cardamoms
- 2 tblsps. peppercorns
- 1 tblsp. mustard seeds
- 10 flakes of garlic
- 2-inch piece of ginger
- 6 green chillies, slit
- 250 grams potatoes, boiled, peeled and cubed
- 1/4 cup vinegar
- Salt to taste

Preparation

Deep fry potatoes to a golden colour. Roast and grind together all spices, chillies, ginger and garlic in vinegar. Heat 6 tblsps. oil and fry the onions to a golden colour. Add pork and fry to a golden colour. Add ground paste and salt. Cover the mixture with hot water. When the pork becomes tender, mix in potatoes and remove the curry from fire. Decorate with coriander leaves.

SPICY PORK CURRY

Ingredients (Serves 8)

- 1 kilo pork, cut into serving portions
- 1/4 cup vinegar
- 2 tblsps. tamarind juice
- 1 tsp. sugar
- 12 red chillies ,12 flakes of garlic
- 1 tblsp dhania-jeera powder
- 1/2 tsp. turmeric powder
- 5 big onions
- 2-inch piece of ginger
- 1 tblsp. peppercorns
- 6 green chillies, slit
- Salt to taste

Preparation

Grind 6 flakes of garlic, half the ginger, red chillies and whole spice to a paste. Heat 5 tblsps. oil and fry the onions, remaining ginger and garlic to a golden colour. Add pork, ground spices, and salt and fry the mixture nicely. Cover it with hot water and cook till the pork is done. Mix in the remaining ingredients and cook till the pork is tender. Serve hot.

Chicken Curry

Ingredients (Serves 6)

- 1 medium chicken, disjointed
- 1 coconut
- 6 red chillies
- 1 tsp. each of saunf, cumin and coriander seeds
- 1/2 tsp. fenugreek seeds
- 6 flakes of garlic, 1 tblsp. peppercorns
- 2 tblsps. poppy seeds, 1/4 tsp. grated nutmeg
- 4 big onions, 2 tblsps. vinegar
- 1 small ball of tamarind
- Salt to taste

Preparation

Roast all the spices and chillies and grind them to a paste. Grate half the coconut and fry it with 2 onions and poppy seeds in oil to a golden colour and grind the mixture to a paste. Extract 2 cups thin and 1/2 cup thick milk from remaining coconut. Cover tamarind with hot water for 5 minutes, then extract its juice. Heat 2 tblsp. each of ghee and oil and fry the remaining onions to a golden colour. Add to this mixture, chicken, salt, spices and ground coconut. Mix nicely, then pour in thin milk and tamarind. Cook over a slow fire till the chicken is tender. Mix in vinegar and thick coconut milk. Decorate with coriander leaves and serve hot.

HEAD CURRY

Ingredients (Serves 4)

- 1 head of goat exclusive of brain
- 1 big onion, 1 tblsp. each of grated ginger and garlic
- 1 lime-sized ball of tamarind
- 150 grams tomatoes
- 1/2 tsp. turmeric powder
- 1 tsp. garam masala
- 6 red chillies, a few curry leaves
- 1 tblsp. dhania-jeera powder
- Salt to taste

Preparation

Clean the head inclusive of tongue, eyes, jaws and cheeks. Cut into pieces and cook adding salt. After the meat is cooked, remove skull bones. Remove skin on tongue, palate and earlobes. Cover tamarind with hot water for 15 minutes and then squeeze out its juice. Heat 4 tblsps. oil and then add the coarsely ground onions, ginger, garlic and curry leaves. Cook them till soft, then add tomatoes, all the spices and salt. When the mixture turns soft, add meat, fry nicely, then add tamarind and one cup of water. Cook for 5 minutes. Serve decorated with coriander leaves.

MUTTON CURRY

Ingredients (Serves 4)

- 500 grams mutton, cut into serving portions
- 1 coconut
- 1 tblsp. coriander seeds, 1 tsp. cumin seeds
- 10 peppercorns, 8 red chillies.
- 1 tsp. garam masala, 1/2 tsp. turmeric powder
- 1 tblsp. poppy seeds
- 1 tblsp. each of grated ginger and garlic
- 2 big onions
- Lime-sized ball of tamarind
- Salt to taste

Preparation

Grind three-fourth of the coconut and extract its thin and thick milk. Fry the remaining coconut and all the whole spices and grind them to a paste with ginger and garlic. Cover tamarind with hot water for 5 minutes and then squeeze out the juice. Heat 4 tblsp. oil and fry the onions to light golden colour. Add mutton and fry it to a red colour. Then put in ground paste and thin coconut milk and tamarind juice. Cook till the mutton is done, put in thick milk, heat and serve decorated with chopped coriander leaves.

EGG AND PEAS CURRY

Ingredients (Serves 2)

- 4 eggs
- 250 grams peas
- 5 flakes of garlic, grated
- 2 medium onions, minced
- 1 tsp. grated ginger
- 1 tsp. garam masala, 1/2 tsp. turmeric powder
- 2 medium potatoes, peeled and sliced
- 2 large tomatoes, pureed
- Handful of coriander leaves
- 4 green chillies, minced
- 3 cups thin and 1 cup thick coconut milk
- Salt and chilli powder to taste

Preparation

Heat 4 tblsps. oil and fry onions, ginger, garlic and chillies till soft. Add all the spices, salt and tomatoes and cook till oil comes out. Then add peas, potatoes and thin coconut milk. When the vegetables turn soft, pour in the thick coconut milk. Now start breaking one egg at a time into the curry after an interval of half a minute, putting each slightly away from the other. Remove the curry after boiling the eggs in it for 5 minutes. Decorate with chopped coriander leaves.

IMPORTANT INGREDIENTS USED IN CURRY PREPARATION AND THEIR MEDICINAL VALUE

Garlic

Garlic is a powerful antiseptic, and therefore it kills bacteria. It improves the voice and eyesight. It is a tonic to the hair and is useful in cough, gastric troubles, worms, heart disease, asthma, acidity, piles, chronic fever, loss of appetite, constipation, diabetes and tuberculosis. It also has properties of reducing high blood pressure.

Ginger

Ginger is good for eyes and throat. A small piece of ginger taken with a pinch of black salt before meals eliminates gas. It gives freedom from cough and cold and is also helpful in cardiac disorders, odema, urinary trouble, jaundice, piles and asthma. Ginger juice is also said to prevent the malignancy of the tongue and the throat. Toothache is also relieved if a piece of ginger is rubbed on the painful tooth.

Onions

From the medicinal point of view, white onions are more beneficial to the body than other varieties. They increase virility and induce sleep. They are good for curing tuberculosis, piles, leprosy, swelling and blood impurities. One is saved from sunstroke if one regularly eats raw onions during hot season. Eating raw onion in the morning and at bedtime is good for jaundice patients.

Coriander leaves

Coriander leaves are mostly used for decorating a dish or preparing chutney. They give a special flavour to food. Coriander is not only fragrant and appetizing but also a good digestive aid. It has a cooling effect on our body, and is good for vision and agreeable to the heart.

Mint

Mint is usually made into chutneys or sometimes put in non-vegetarian dishes. It is not only palatable and appetizing but is also good for heart. It expels gas and is useful in cough, dysentery, gastroenteritis and diarrhoea.

Vegetables

They are extremely rich source of minerals, enzymes and vitamins. Their nutritional value varies according to their different parts. Leaves, stems and fruits are rich sources of minerals, vitamins, water and roughage, whereas seeds are high in carbohydrates and proteins. Greener and fresher the vegetables, higher their vitamin content. Therefore always go in for fresh vegetables available in the market.

Eggs

Eggs are a valuable source of animal proteins and next to milk in providing nutrition. Egg yolk contains Iron, B vitamins, calcium and a considerable amount of proteins. White portion contains vitamin B and more than half the amount of proteins in egg. Patients of high cholesterol and heart disease should not eat yolks but go only for whites of the egg.

Fish

Fish rates high in nutritional value. It supplies proteins which are more easily digestible than the proteins of meat. Fish gives fat, vitamins A & D and minerals like iodine and copper to the body. Fish is a low-fat form of proteins. Sardines, mackerel and other oily fish contain omega-3 fatty acids that help clear the body of cholesterol.

Meat & Poultry

These are very rich sources of proteins. Besides proteins they are rich in fats, vitamin A and phosphorus. However, kidney and liver are low in fat. Just one helping a day of meat or fish is enough for the daily body requirement of proteins.

FOODGRAINS Cookery Glossary

English	Spiked millet	Barley	Jowar	Italian millet	Maize (dry)	Oatmeal	Ragi
Hindi	Bajra	Jau	Juar-janera	Kangri	Makai	Jai	Okra
Tamil	Cambu	Barli arisi	Cholam	Thenai	Muka cholam	—	Ragi
Telugu	Gantelu	Barli biyyam	Jonnalu	Korralu	Mekka jonnalu	—	Chollu
Marathi	Bajri	Juv	Jwari	Rala	Muka	—	Nachni
Bengali	Bajra	Job	Juar	Syamadhan kangni	Sukna paka bhutta	Jai	—
Gujarati	Bajri	Jau	Juar	Ral kang	Makai	—	Ragi bhav
Malayalam	Kamboo	Yavam	Cholam	Thina	Unakku cholam	Oat mavu	Moothari (korra)
Kannada	—	—	Jola	—	Vonugida musikinu	Jolu	Ragi
Kashmiri	Baajr'u	Wushku	—	Shol	Makka'y	—	—

Contd...

English	Rice (raw)	Rice (parboiled)	Rice (white)	Rice (black)	Rice flakes	Rice (puffed)	Samai
Hindi	Arwa chawal	Usna chawal	Safed chawal	Chaval (kala)	Chowla	Murmura	Kutki, Samwali
Tamil	Pachai arisi	Puzhungal arisi	Vellai puttu arisi	Karuppu puttu arisi	Arisi aval	Arisia pori	Samai
Telugu	Pachi biyyam	Uppudu biyyam	Thella biyyam	Nalla biyyam	Atukulu	Murmuralu	—
Marathi	Tandool	Tandool ukda	—	—	Pohe	Murmure	Sava
Bengali	Atap chowl	Siddha chowl	—	—	Chaler khood	Muri	Kangni
Gujarati	Hatna	Ukadelloo chokha	—	—	Pohva	Mumra	—
Malayalam	Pacchari	Puzhungal ari	Velutha puttari	Krutha puttari	Avil	Pori	—
Kannada	Kotnuda	Kotnuda	—	—	Avalukki	—	Puri
Kashmiri	—	—	—	—	—	—	—

Contd...

English	Semolina	Vermicelli	Wheat (whole)	Wheat flour (whole)	Wheat flour (refined)	Wheat (broken)
Hindi	Sooji	Siwain	Gehun	Atta	Maida	Daliya
Tamil	Ravai	Semiya	Godumai	Muzhu godnai ma	Maida mavu	Godhumbi ravai
Telugu	Rawa	Semiya	Godhumalu	Godhum pindi	Maidha pindi	Dinchina gadhumalu
Marathi	–	Shevaya	Gahu	Gahu kuneek	Gahu kuneek	Gavache satva
Bengali	Suji	Sewai	Gomasta	Atta	Maida	Bhanga gom
Gujarati	–	–	Ghau	Ato	–	Fadia ghaun
Malayalam	Rava	Semiya	Muzhu gothambu	Gothambu mavu	Maidu tha gothambu mavu	Gothumbu ari
Kannada	–	Shavige	Godhi	Godhi	Hittu madia	Kuttida Godhi
Kashmiri	–	Ku' nu'	–	–	–	–

VEGETABLES

English	Ash gourd	Bitter gourd	Bottle gourd	Brinjal	Broad beans	Cabbage	Capsicum
Hindi	Safed petha	Karela	Ghia	Baingan	Sem	Bandhgobi	Simla mirch
Bengali	Chal kumdo	karala	Laoo	Begoon	Sheem	Badha kopee	Lonka
Assamese	Lao bishesh	–	Jati lao	Bengena	Urahi	Bondhakobi	Kashmiri jalakai
Oriya	Pani kakkaru	–	Lau	Baigana	Shimba	Patrokobi	Simla lonka
Marathi	Kohala	Karle	Dudhi	Wangi	Chewda	Pan kobi	Bhopli mirchi
Gujarati	Petha	Karela	Dudhi	Ringna	Papdi	Kobi	Simla marchan
Telugu	Boodie gumadi	Kakara	Sorakaya	Vankaya	Pedda chikkudu	Kosu	Pedda mirappa
Kannada	Budu gumbala	Hagalkai	Sorekai	Badanekai	Chapparadavare	Kosu	Donne minasinakai
Tamil	Pooshanikkai	Pavakkai	Suraikai	Kaththarikai	Avaraikai	Muttaikosu	Kuda milakai
Malayalam	Kumbalanga	Kaypakka	Cheraikai	Vazhutheninga	Amarakai	Muttakose	Parangi mulagu
Kashmiri	Masha'ly al	Karelu	–	Waangun	–	Bandgobhi	–

Contd...

English	Carrot	Cauliflower	Cluster beans	Colocasia	Coriander leaves	Cucumber	Curry leaves
Hindi	Gajar	Phulgobi	Guar ki phalli	Arvi	Hara Dhania	Khira	Kadi patta
Bengali	Gujar	Foolcopy	Jhar sim	—	Dhonay pata	Sasha	Curry pata
Assamese	Gajor	Phoolkobi	—	Kochu	Dhania paat	—	Narasingha paat
Oriya	Gajar	Phulakobi	—	—	Dhania patra	—	Bhrusanga patta
Marathi	Gajar	Fulkobi	Govari	Alu kanda	Kothimbir	Kakari	Kadhi patta
Gujarati	Gajar	Fool kobi	Govar	Alvi	Kothmir	Kakdi	Mitho limdo
Telugu	Gajara	Cauliflower	Goruchikkudu kayalu	Chamadumpa	Kothimeera	Dosakaya	Karivepaku
Kannada	Gajari	Hookosu	Gorikayi	Keshave	Kottambari soppu	Southaikayi	Karibevu
Tamil	Carrot	Koveppu	Kothavarangai	Seppann kizhangu	Koththamali ilaigal	Kakkarikkai	Kariveppilai
Malayalam	Carrot	Coliflower	Kothavara	Chembu	Kothamalli ila	Vellari	Kariveppila
Kashmiri	—	Phoolgobhi	—	—	—	Laa'r	—

Contd...

English	Drumstick	French beans	Garlic	Ginger (fresh)	Green chillies	Jackfruit	Lady's finger
Hindi	Sahjan ki phali	Pharsbeen	Lassan	Adrak	Hari mirch	Kathal	Bhindi
Bengali	Sajane dauta	French beans	Rasoon	Ada (tatka)	Kancha lonka	Echore	Dhanroce
Assamese	Sajina	Faras been	Naharoo	Ada (kesa)	Kesa jalakia	—	Bhendi
Oriya	Sajana chhuin	French beans	Rasuna	Ada (kancha)	Kancha lonka	—	Bhendi
Marathi	Shevgyachya shenga	Farasbi	Lasun	Aale	Hirvya mirchya	Kawla phanas	Bhendi
Gujarati	Saragvani shing	Fansi	Lasan	Adu	Lila marcha	Phunas	Bhinda
Telugu	Munagakayalu	French chikkudu	Vellulli	Allam (pachchi)	Pachchi mirapakayalu	Letha panasa	Bendakaaya
Kannada	Nuggekai	Avare	Bellulli	Ashi Shunti	Hasi menasinakai	Yele halasu	Bendekai
Tamil	Murungaikai	Beans	Ulli Poondu	Inji	Pachchai milagai	Pila pinchu	Vendaikai
Malayalam	Muringakkaya	Beans	Veluthulli	Inji	Pachamulagu	Idichakka	Vendakka
Kashmiri	—	—	Ruhan	—	Myool martsu waungun	—	Bindu

Contd...

English	Lettuce	Lemon	Mint leaves	Onion	Parwal	Peas	Plantain flower	Plantain green
Hindi	Salad ke patte	Nimbu	Pudina	Pyaz	Parwal	Matar	Kele ka phool	Kacha kela
Bengali	Lettuce	Lebu	Poodina pata	Pyaz	Potol	Motor	Mocha	Kancha kala
Assamese	Laipaat	Nemu	Podina	–	Patol	Motormah	–	–
Oriya	Lettuce	Lembu	Podana patra	–	Potala	Matar	–	–
Marathi	Saladchi paane	Limbu	Pudina	Kanda	–	Matar	Kel phool	Kele
Gujarati	Lettuce	Limbu	Fudino	Dungli	–	Vatana	Kelphool	Kela
Telugu	Lettuce koora	Nimma	Pudhina koora	Nirulli	–	Bathanedu	Aratipuwu	Arati kayi
Kannada	Lettuce soppu	Nimbu	Pudina sopu	Erulli	–	Betani	Balo mothu	Bala kayi
Tamil	Lettuce keerai	Elumicham pazham	Pudhinaa	Vengayam	–	Pattani	Vazhaippu	Vazhaikkai
Malayalam	Uvarcheera	Cherunaranga	Pudhinaa	Ulli	–	Pattani Payaru	Vazhappoo	Vazhakka
Kashmiri	Salaad	–	–	Gandu	–	Matar	–	–

Contd...

English	Plantain stem	Potato	Radish	Red pumpkin	Ridge gourd	Snake gourd	Sweet potato	Yam elephant
Hindi	Kele ka tana	Aloo	Muli	Sitaphal	Torai	–	Shakarkand	Zaminkand
Bengali	Thor	Aloo	Mulo	Ronga Koomra	Jhinge	Chichinga	Rangalu	Zaminkand
Assamese	–	Alu	–	Ronga lao	–	–	–	Kham aloo
Oriya	–	Alu	–	Kakharu	–	–	–	Kaath aloo
Marathi	Kelecha khunt	Batate	Mula	Lal bhopla	Dodka	Pudwal	Ratale	Deshi alu
Gujarati	Kelanu thed	Batata	Mula	Kolu	Turai	Pandola	Sakkaria	Suran
Telugu	Arati davva	Bangaala dumpa	Mullangi	Erra gummadi	Beerakai	Potlakayi	Dumpalu	Suran
Kannada	Dindu	Aalugadde	Mullangi	Kempu kumbala	Heeraikai	Padavalai	Genasu	Kanda dumpa
Tamil	Vazhaithandu	Urulaikizhangu	Mullangi	Parangikai	Pirrkkankai	Podalangai	Sarkarai valli kizhangu	Suvarnagadde
Malayalam	Vazhappindi	Uralakkizhangu	Mullangi	Chuvappu mathan	Pecchinga	Padavalanga	Chakkara kizhangu	Chenai kizhangu
Kashmiri	–	Oloo	Muj	Paanmal	Turrelu	–	–	Chena

PULSES

English	Bengal gram (whole)	Bengal gram (split)	Black gram (split)	Black gram (whole)	Cornflour	Cow gram	Green gram (whole)
Hindi	Chana	Chana dal	Urad dal	Sabat urad	Makai ka atta	Lobia (bada)	Moong
Bengali	Chola	Banglar chhola	Mashkolair dal	Mashkolai dal	Bhoottar maida	Barbati	Mug
Assamese	–	Buttor dail	Matir dail (phola)	Matir dail (gota)	Moida	–	–
Oriya	–	Buta (chhota)	Biri (phala)	Biri (gota)	Makka atta	–	–
Marathi	Hurbhura	Chana dal	Udid dal	Udid	Makyache pith	Kuleeth	Mug
Gujarati	Chana	Chana nidaal	Adad ni dal	Adad	Makai no lot	–	Mag
Telugu	Sanagalu	Senaga pappu	Mina pappu	Minu mulu	Mokkajonnalu (pindi)	Ada chandalu	Pesalu
Kannada	Kadale	Kadale bela	Uddina bela	Uddu	Musukinajolada hittu	Thadaguni	Hesaru kalu
Tamil	Muzhu kadalai	Kadalai paruppu	Ulutham paruppu	Ulundhu	Chola Maavu	Karamani	Pachai payaru
Malayalam	Kadala	Kadala parippu	Uzhunnu parrippu	Uzhunnu	Cholapodi	Payar	Cherupayaru
Kashmiri	Chanu	–	Maha	–	–	–	Muang

Contd...

English	Green gram (split)	Horse gram	Kesari dal	Kidney beans	Red gram	Red lentils	Soya bean
Hindi	Moong dal	Kulthi	Lang dal	Rajma	Arhar dal	Masoor dal	Bhat
Bengali	–	Kulthi kalai	Khesari	Barbati beej	Arhar dal	Lal masoor (bhanga)	Gari kalai
Assamese	–	–	–	Markhowa urahi	Rahor dail	Masoor dail (phola)	–
Oriya	–	–	–	Baragudi chhuin	Harada dali	Masura dali (phala)	–
Marathi	–	Kuleeth	Lakh dal	–	Tur dal	Masur dal	Soya
Gujarati	–	Kuleeth	Lakh	–	Tuver dal	Masur dal	Soya
Telugu	Pesaru pappu	Ulavalu	Lamka pappu	–	Kandi pappu	Missu pappu	–
Kannada	Hesare bele	Huruli	–	–	Togar bele	Masur bele	–
Tamil	Pasi paruppu	Kollu	Vattuparuppu	–	Thuvaram parappu	Massor paruppu	–
Malayalam	Cherupayar parippu	Muthira	–	–	Thuvara parippu	Masoor parippu	Soya bean
Kashmiri	–	–	–	–	–	Musur	–

FRUITS AND DRY FRUITS

English	Almond	Coconut	Currants	Dates	Dry plums
Hindi	Badam	Nariyal	Mungaqqa	Khajur	Alu bukhara
Bengali	Badam	Narcole	Manaca	Khejoor	Sookno kool
Assamese	Badam	Narikol	Kismis	Khejur	Sukan bogori
Oriya	Badaam	Nadia	Kala kismis	Khajura	Barakoli jateeya phala
Marathi	Badam	Naral	Manuka	Khajur	Alubhukar
Gujarati	Badam	Naliyer	Kalli draksh	Khajoor	Suka Plum
Telugu	Badam	Kobbari kaaya	Endu nalla dhraksha	Kharjoora pandu	–
Kannada	Badami	Tenginakai	Dweepa dharakshi-kappu	Kharjoora	–
Tamil	Badam/vadhumai	Thengai	Karumdhraakshai	Perichampazham	Aalpacota ular pazham
Malayalam	Badam	Nalikeram/Thenga	Karuthamurthiri	Eethapazham	–

Contd...

English	Guavas	Lemon	Orange	Raisins	Walnuts
Hindi	Amrud	Nimbu	Santra	Kishmish	Akhrot
Bengali	Payara	Lebu	Kamla lebu	Kishmish	Akhrot
Assamese	Madhurium	Nemu	Sumothira	Sukan angoor	Akhrot
Oriya	Pijuli	Lembu	Kamala	Kismis	Akhrot
Marathi	Peru	Limbu	Santre	Bedane	Akrod
Gujarati	Jamrukh	Limbu	Santara	Lal draksh	Akhrot
Telugu	Jaamapandu	Nimma	Kamala Pandu	Kismis pallu	Aakrot
Kannada	Seebe	Nimbe	Kittale	Dweepadrakshi	Acrota
Tamil	Koyyapazham	Elumicham pazham	Kichilipazham	Ular dhraakshai	Akhrot
Malayalam	Perakkai	Cherunaranga	Madhura naranga	Unakkamunthiri	Akrotandi

Contd...

DRY SPICES

English	Aniseed	Asafoetida	Basil leaves	Bay leaf	Caraway seeds	Cardamom (brown)	Cardamom (green)	Cinnamon
Hindi	Saunf	Hing	Tulse ke patte	Tej patta	Shahjeera	Moti elaichi	Choti elaichi	Dalchini
Bengali	Mowri	Hing	Tulsi pata	Tej pata	Sajeera	Elach (tamate)	Elach (sobooj)	Daroochini
Assamese	Guwamori	Hing	Tulosi paat	Tejpaat	Bilati jira	Ilachi (muga)	Ilachi (sevjia)	Dalcheni
Oriya	Panamahuri	Hengu	Tulasi patra	Teja patra	Sahajira	Aleicha	Gijuratie	Dalachini
Marathi	Badishep	Hing	Tulsichi paney	Tamal patra	Shahjeera	Masala welchi	Welchi (hirvi)	Dalchini
Gujarati	Variyali	Hing	Tulsina pan	Tamal patra	Jiru	Elcho	Lila alchi	Tuj
Telugu	Sopaginja	Inguva	Thulasi akulu	—	Seema sopyginjale	Yalakulu	Yala kulu (pachavi)	Dalchina chekka
Kannada	Sopubeeja	Hingu	Tulasi ele	—	Caraway beejagalre	Yalakki	Yalakki (hasuru)	Dalchini
Tamil	Perumjeerakam	Perungaayam	Thulasi	—	Karunjeerakam	Elakkai (Pazhuppu)	Elakkai (pachchai)	Lavangapattai
Malayalam	Perumjeerakam	Kaayam	Tulasi	—	Karunjeerakam	Elakkaya	Pach Elakkaya	Karuvapatta
Kashmiri	—	Yangu	—	—	—	Aal budu'a aal	—	—

Contd...

English	Cloves	Coriander seeds	Cumin seeds	Fenugreek seeds	Mace	Mustard seeds	Nutmeg	Parsley
Hindi	Laung	Sukha dhania	Jeera	Methi dana	Javitri	Rai	Jaiphal	Ajmooda ka patta
Bengali	Labango	Dhonay	Jeera	Methi	Jaeetri	Sarsay	Jaifall	Parsley
Assamese	Long	Dhania guti	Gota jeera	Paleng	Janee	Sarioh guti	Jaaiphal	Sugandhi lota
Oriya	Labanga	Dhania	Jira	Methi	Jayatree	Sorisha	Jaiphala	Balabalua shaga
Marathi	Lavanga	Dhane	Jire	Methi dane	Jaypatri	Mohari	Jayphal	Ajmoda
Gujarati	Laving	Dhana	Jeeru	Methi	Jaypatra	Rai	Jaypal	Ajmo
Telugu	Lavangalu	Dhaniyalu	Jeelakara	Menthulu	Japatra	Aavaalu	Jaikaaya	Kothimeerajati koora
Kannada	Lavanga	Kottambari beeja	Jeerige	Menthe	Japathri	Sasive kalu	Jaika	Kottambari jotiya soppu
Tamil	Kraambu	Koththamali virai	Jeerakam	Vendhayam	Jaadipathri	Kadugu	Jaadhikai	Kothamalu ilaigal pole
Malayalam	Karayaamboovu	Kothamalli	Jeerakam	Uluva	Jathipathri	Kadugu	Jathikka	Malliela pole
Kashmiri	Ru'ang	Daaniwal	Zyur	—	Jalwatur	—	Zaaphal	—

English	Peppercorns	Pomegranate seeds	Poppy seeds	Red Chillies	Tamarind	Turmeric	Vinegar	Thymol
Hindi	Kali mirch ke daane	Anardana	Khus khus	Lal mirch	Imli	Haldi	Sirka	Ajwain
Bengali	Marich	Dareem bij	Posto	Paka lonka	Tentool	Halood	Seerka	–
Assamese	Jaluk	Dalim guti	–	Sukan jalakia	Teteli	Halodhi	Sirika	–
Oriya	Golamaricha	Dalimba manji	–	Nali lankamaricha	Tentuli	Haladi	Vinegar	–
Marathi	Kale Miri	Dalimbache dane	Khas khas	Lal mirchya	Chincha	Halad	Sirka	Onva
Gujarati	Mari	Dadamna bee	Khaskhas	Lal marcha	Amli	Haldar	Sirko	–
Telugu	Miriyaalu	Daanimma ginjalu	Gasagasaalu	Erra mirapa kayalu	Chinthapandu	Pasupu	–	–
Kannada	Menasina kalu	Dalimbo beeja	Gasagase beeja	Kempu menasinakai	Hunase hannu	Arasina	–	–
Tamil	Milagu	Maadhulai vidhai	Kasakasaa	Milagai vatal	Puli	Manjal	Pulikaadi	–
Malayalam	Kurumulagu	Madhala naranga kuru	Kaskas	Chuvanna Mulagu	Puli	Manjal	Vinagiri	–

Also Available
in Hindi

Also Available
in Hindi

Also Available
in Kannada, Tamil

Also Available
in Kannada

Also Available
in Kannada

STRESS MANAGEMENT

All books available at www.vspublishers.com

Also Available in Hindi

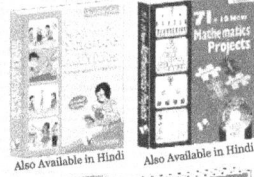

Also Available in Hindi

Also Available in Hindi

PUZZLES

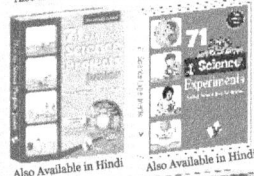

Also Available in Hindi

Also Available in Hindi

DRAWING BOOKS

Also Available in Hindi

Also Available in Hindi, Tamil & Bangla

CHILDREN'S ENCYCLOPEDIA – THE WORLD OF KNOWLEDGE

Contact us at sales@vspublishers.com